IDEAS · IN
STENCILLING

A DESAINT

STUDIO EDITIONS
LONDON

First published 1927 by
Charles Griffin & Co. Ltd., London

This edition published 1990 by
Studio Editions Ltd, Princess House,
50 Eastcastle Street, London W1N 7AP
England

Printed and bound in Hong Kong

ISBN 1 85170 408 6

PREFACE.

STENCILLING for decorative purposes has a fascination and a charm peculiarly its own and appeals strongly to the craftsman of artistic temperament. It admits of individuality of treatment and of endless variety of design suitable in its application to unpretentious dwelling-houses as well as to stately mansions with large and lofty rooms ; to spacious business premises with boardrooms and suites of offices ; to large hotels with splendid halls for banquets and dances ; to the magnificent buildings of " Clubland," or the princely saloons of Ocean Liners. It serves also most admirably for the delicate manipulation necessary to the chaste requirements in interiors of ecclesiastical edifices.

Stencilling has gained for itself a large place in the education of every good craftsman and its technique is part of his stock in trade. The standard work on " Painting and Decorating " by Walter J. Pearce* gives precise and clear instructions in regard to the cutting of stencils, the manipulation of tools and application of Colours, whilst in regard to the scientific principles of colour work Hurst's " Painter's Colours, Oils and Varnishes "* is part of every house-decorator's upmake.

The Author's intention in this present work is to supply IDEAS IN STENCILLING, the outcome of many years' experience of work upon a variety of buildings in Great Britain and in France. The success of stencilled ornament depends largely upon the combination of colourings in the design, and it is often in this particular that the skilled artisan is deficient. Effects are not infrequently robbed of their beauty by the use of colours which offend the eye, and it is to safeguard this and the consequent disappointment that the author has carefully elaborated the KEY-PLATE of colourings which form the basis of this work.

This KEY-PLATE contains FORTY TINTS which have been selected with the utmost care from numerous effects and the tints are numbered. Many choice designs are included in the book and numbers indicate the colours to be used in agreement with the Key-plate. By the application of colours corresponding with the tints shewn the most charming effects will be secured. All the combinations of " Colorations " are the results of the most exacting tests and are submitted with confidence to craftsmen whose experience in harmonising colours is limited. They may be quite sure of achieving success.

Other handicraftsmen besides those engaged in house decorating will find this colour Key-plate and its application of the greatest service. It will prove useful in the ceramic industry for oramental pottery and tiles, to glass embossers, bookbinders, and others who apply the decorative art to fabrics, silk, velvet, satin, and to paper, as well as to many domestic articles.

The author is gratified that Charles Griffin & Company, Ltd., who have gained international fame as publishers of technical books, have added this to their catalogue.

A. DESAINT.

PARIS, March, 1927.

LIST OF PLATES.

Ideas in Stencilling.

Material for Stencil Plates.—In making stencil plates for various kinds of work, paper or metal are employed. Willisden paper is a good paper for large stencils, such as are often required for churches and public buildings. It is a patent paper, extra stout, and it is somewhat hard in cutting, but durable when in use, and repaying the little extra labour involved in cutting ; it is made only in one width, 58 inches, in continuous rolls, and sold at 1s. 6d. per yard run.

" Whatman " papers are very suitable for stencil making, but being hand made they are rather expensive. They are sold in sheets of definite sizes.

Imperial, 30 inches by 22 inches.
Double Elephant, 40 inches by 27 inches.

Tinfoil makes good stencils, but it is more expensive than paper, it cuts easily with a sharp knife. Tinfoil stencils cannot be repaired when broken, but they lie flatly on the wall.

Stencils cut out of sheet zinc are useful when the plate is to be used a certain number of times ; its weight keeps it steady while in use.

The stencil pattern may be drawn directly upon the paper out of which the pattern is to be cut. Few artists draw the design direct on the stencil paper, for rubbing out and alterations weaken the paper ; it may also be drawn upon cartoon paper and then traced or transferred to the stencil paper, or again, it may be drawn on thin paper and transferred by the aid of carbonised or copying paper.

Preparation of the Paper.—Whatever paper is selected for the stencil, it should be saturated with linseed oil until it becomes transparent and allowed to dry throughout; this operation gives the paper additional toughness, retains pliancy, and adds a waterproof quality. When the stencil is cut, the paper must be finally knotted with two coats of patent shellac knotting, to prevent it from absorbing the colour.

Stencil Cutting.—Having prepared the paper, the process of cutting out will be found to demand the greatest care; well ground and sharpened knives are necessary (see Figs. 1, 2, 3, 4); oil stone should be within reach, for it is quite useless attempting to work with a blunt knife.

Lay the prepared stencil paper on a large piece of polished plate glass, and commence cutting out with the point of the knife, keeping the tip of the forefinger constantly pressed upon the back of the blade, be careful the plate glass is always under the paper when the knife is in operation, commence at the top left-hand corner of the design and be careful not to cut too far; do not attempt to cut a stencil by *fixing* the paper over the glass plate and moving your own position to meet the constantly changing direction of the knife. The left hand must move the stencil in various directions, in sympathy with the movements of the knife.

Perforations of a circular form are made by the use of a punch (Fig. 5), punches are made in various sizes (Fig. 6), gouges are also used for particular shapes. It is not necessary to strike the punch except for extra thick papers, a firm pressure of the hand is generally sufficient for the purpose required, slightly turning the wrist at the same time. For this operation, a sheet of tin or lead must be substituted for the plate glass. Punching can also be done on a block of lead,

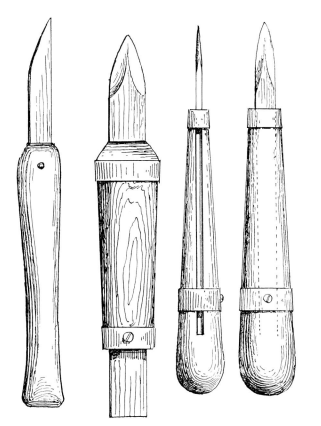
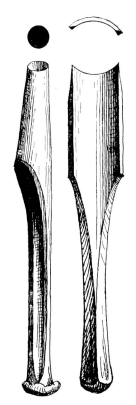

Fig. 1.   Fig. 2.   Fig. 3.   Fig. 4.   Fig. 5.   Fig. 6.

Fig. 7.

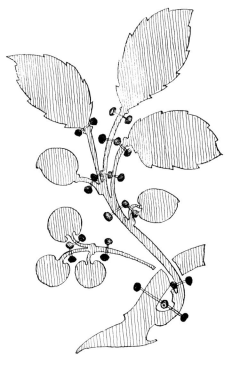

Fig. 8.

one inch thick and a few inches square, and in order to enable the sharp punch to cut out neatly through the paper, without damaging its own edge ; a single tap with a light hammer is sufficient.

Ties.—A sufficient number of ties are reserved, that is bands crossing the openings at intervals and serving to hold the plate firmly together (Fig. 7), thus preventing various parts of the design from curling, twisting or tearing. It is afterwards necessary to go over the work, to fill the blanks left by the ties, using a camel hair or red sable pencil. This is a rather difficult operation, because it is almost impossible to get the same shade when painted by hand as with the same colour stencilled.

The majority of stencilled work now remains untouched, that is to say, the design is entirely cut out, and held with ties of very fine iron or brass wires (Fig. 8) affixed on different parts of the stencil to keep the intricate details from being destroyed during the process of stencilling. It must be understood that iron or brass ties are to be placed on the side of the stencil furthest from the wall or surface under treatment—*i.e.*, the side of the stencil which receives the colour. Wire or brass ties are fixed to the stencil with glue or wax ; if glue is used it must be covered up with paper.

The use of Stencil Plates.—The stencil being laid in its proper place, stencil pins (Figs. 9 and 10) are used to keep it in correct position while work is proceeding. Pins must not be placed in conspicuous places, as the small holes made by them cannot be easily hidden afterwards.

The paint must be mixed fairly thick, and well strained.

The author recommends the tube colours, for colours not well ground are never as brilliant as they should be.

Stencils brushes (Figs. 11, 12, and 13) must not be too small, for if they are so, the work does not go on quickly, and the colour is apt to work under the stencil.

A good broad brush covers a stencil in half the time as compared with a small one. However, when using two distinct colours in the same plate, brushes must not be too large, otherwise one colour will work into the other.

The stencil brush must be clean and dry to begin with. In filling the brush, it should be dipped in the colour and then knocked on the side of the palette once or twice to distribute the colour evenly over the surface of the brush. Hold the brush between the thumb and the middle finger of the right hand, with the first finger resting on the top of the butt end. It is important to keep the brush quite perpendicular (*i.e.*, at right angles with the stencil plate). Just dab the brush over the whole stencil, and when the colour has been worked out to a certain extent, gently hammer the brush over the stencil plate; never rub the paint on as by the ordinary movement of plain surface painting, it would work the colour under the stencil and ruin the work; another cause of colour working under the stencil is, if, when the brush is freshly charged with colour, it be used too heavily in one place. Remember to dab the brush over the whole stencil as mentioned in the preceding lines.

When stencil plates are used for several colours it is an advantage to use masks to cover the openings and to prevent the brush touching the parts where colour is not wanted, these masks can be easily pinned over the stencil. Sometimes, in case of small designs, it is easier to keep them in position with the hand.

Fig. 9. Fig. 10.

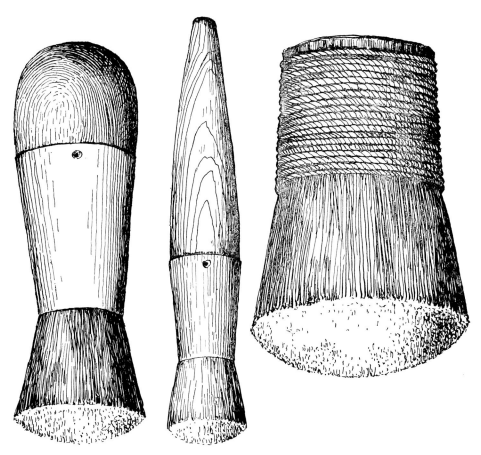

Fig. 11.   Fig. 12.   Fig. 13.

A minute inspection for omissions is advisable before removing the stencil plate, for it would be hazardous to attempt to replace the plate over wet paint.

To remove the plate without injury to the work, with the left hand raise the plate by an unfixed corner, remove the pins with the right hand, and lift the plate away at the same time as the last pin is removed, in this way it is possible to avoid sliding the plate over the wet work.

It is necessary to wipe the back of the stencils occasionally, and to clean the stencil entirely at times ; otherwise the finer portions of the stencil will get filled up with colour.

Care of Stencils.—Stencils out of use must be left clean. To attain this, they are laid flat on a clean sheet of paper and first cleaned with the stencil brush, using turpentine, then they are dabbed with a cloth and put away in a drawer between two sheets of stout paper.

Stencilling in Distemper.—There is no reason why stencil patterns should not be made in distemper.

Decorating and stencilling in distemper are at first a little troublesome, for several reasons :

1. Because it is difficult to estimate the value of the colours when using. To obviate this, try the tints on paper and dry them slowly before a fire, so that the final effect can be estimated.

2. When the stencil plate has become saturated by gradual absorption of water from the distemper it curls ; this is called " sagging." This difficulty could be overcome by using metal stencil plates ; but metal is too heavy to be pinned to a wall, and it does not accommodate itself

so well as paper stencil plates to the irregularities of the walls. Therefore, the stencil plate to be used in distemper must be cut out of paper well soaked in oil and coated three or four times with knotting. It would be advisable for the decorator to have two plates of the same design, ceasing to use one at the first sign of " sagging," and cleaning off from the stencil the accumulated distemper, and placing over it a piece of stout board, weighted by a book, until it is dry, after which a coat of knotting should be applied.

3. The tendency of the stencil colour to soften and mix with the ground colour on which it is applied, and so to cause it to become " shady " in drying. To obviate this difficulty, the distemper *ground* must contain size of sufficient strength added hot, while the colours *for stencilling* should contain a weaker size added cold. This makes the latter work more freely and with consequently less rapid absorption.

Never use oil or tube colours over distemper. The oil would spread out into the size ground and leave unsightly edges.

Stencilling on Washable Distemper.—In the case of washable distempers upon which designs are to be stencilled, three or four days must elapse after grounding before stencilling is commenced.

Stencilling on New Plaster.—If stencilling on new plaster is required, leaving as background the natural colour of the plaster, only earth pigments should be used, in order to avoid the reaction of the lime in the plaster upon the colours.

Stencilling on Canvas, Velvet, Silk, and other Textile Fabrics.

—Prepared canvas Burlaps, Anaglypta, and other decorative materials, such as Fabricona, etc., can be stencilled with pigments in oil ; but for velvets, silks, cloth, or any other choice textile materials, specially-prepared " textile stencilling colours " must be procured. These " lay-on " easily, do not spread under the stencil, or stain the fabric around their edges. Soft goods, curtains and other draperies, should be stretched over a flat surface, such as a table top or drawing board.

Stencilling with Aerograph.

—Aerographs or air brushes are spray diffusers worked by compressed air from machine air pumps. Spray-work produces a texture much finer than stippling. Oil paints, distemper, water colours, stains and dyes can all be used for this process, but in a more diluted condition than for brush work. Unique effects can be obtained. Colours can be blended and graded in any medium and on any surface in a most remarkable way, which can be fully appreciated. One tint is put over another without waiting for the first to dry, and no washing-up or muddy tints are produced. Spray work is valuable for wall-paper stencilling, show cards and for making picture and Christmas cards. It is specially valuable for decorating all classes of textile fabrics, as it does not interfere with the texture in any way, this latter never being warped or the weft closed up as by brush work, and the pile of velvet is not matted or laid flat.

COLOURS.

Nothing is more important to the decorator than a keen appreciation of colours, though in many instances this consideration is set aside, and good work disfigured by an injudicious arrangement of tints.

The Author cannot undertake to deal exhaustively with the theory of colour, but for the purpose of this book essential matters are set out below.

Colours are classed under three heads :—

> PRIMARY : blue, red, yellow ;
> SECONDARY : purple, green, orange ;
> TERTIARY : olive, russet, citron.

Two of the primaries mixed produce a perfect secondary colour which harmonizes with the remaining primary.

Thus, blue and yellow form green, which harmonizes with red ; yellow and red produce orange, which harmonizes with blue ; red and blue produce purple which harmonizes with yellow.

By mixing in pairs the secondary colours obtained from the primaries, then is produced a third order of colours called tertiary colours ; thus, if green is mixed with orange they will form citrine or citron colour ; in mixing orange with purple, they will form russet ; and if purple is mixed with green, they will form olive colour.

Thus, citron, russet and olive constitute the third order of colours, each of which is variously compounded of the three original or primary colours, as the second order is of two, the primary order being single and uncompounded ; and lastly by duly mixing the three orders of colours, black will be produced, terminating the series in neutrality of colour.

By the varied admixture of these colours is produced the infinity of hues, shades and tints which abound in works of art.

By a disproportionate mixture of the three colours of either order or of the whole together we produce the hues usually called dirty or brown. The browns are a valuable class of colours of warm hues, there are red and yellow browns, and browns are of all hues except blue, which is a cold colour affording a useful class of greys, being the contrast to brown.

Primary colours may be altered by mixing them in varied proportions, then all hues of colours are produced, when these hues are diluted with white they form *tints*, when they are toned with black they form different *shades* of colour.

If a hue contains much white, it is said to be light; if a shade contains much black, it is said to be dark.

The metaphorical expressions, warm and cold, are also applied to colours; warm colours are red, orange and yellow; cold colours are green, blue and violet.

MIXING TINTS TO THE KEY PLATE.

The colours used for each mixture are indicated in the order of their proportions; that is to say, the first colour mentioned is that of which the most is required and the last is that of which the smallest quantity is wanted.

When a tint is composed of three or four colours, it follows that the last enters into it in a less degree than the first, and the third in a greater degree than the fourth or last.

No. 1—White, Chrome-yellow (light), Yellow ochre.

No. 2—White, Ultramarine (deep), Veronese green.

No. 3—White, Raw umber, Chrome-yellow (deep).

No. 4—White, Vermilion, Crimson lake, Yellow ochre.

No. 5—White, Madder lake (deep), Burnt sienna.

No. 6—Crimson lake, Vandyke brown, White.

No. 7—Burnt sienna, Chrome-yellow (orange), White.

No. 8—White, Chrome-yellow (light), Chrome-green (light), Raw umber.

No. 9—White, Emerald-green, Yellow ochre, Burnt umber.

No. 10—White, Emerald-green, Chrome-yellow (deep), Raw umber.

No. 11—White, Chrome-yellow (light), Raw umber.

No. 12—White, Burnt sienna, Chrome-yellow (light), Veronese green.

No. 13—White, Prussian blue, Yellow ochre.

No. 14—Emerald-green, Ivory black, White, Ultramarine (deep).

No. 15—White, Ivory black, Chrome-yellow (deep), Burnt sienna.

No. 16—Burnt sienna, Burnt umber, Chrome-yellow (deep), White.

No. 17—Chrome-yellow (deep), Vandyke brown, White.

No. 18—White, Chrome-yellow (orange), Emerald-green.

No. 19—Chrome-green (light), Chrome-yellow (orange), White.

No. 20—Crimson lake, Yellow ochre, White.

No. 21—White, Crimson lake, Yellow ochre.

No. 22—White, Ivory black, Chrome-yellow (deep).

No. 23—Cadmium (light), Ivory black, White.

No. 24—White, Prussian blue, Crimson lake.

No. 25—White, Burnt umber, Chrome-yellow (deep).

No. 26—Raw sienna, White, Ivory black.

No. 27—Burnt umber, White, Emerald-green, Yellow ochre.

No. 28—White, Raw umber, Rose madder.

No. 29—Chrome-green (light), Ivory black, Raw umber, White.

No. 30—White, Chrome-green (light), Chrome-yellow (deep), Yellow ochre.

No. 31—White, Ivory black, Crimson lake, Yellow ochre.

No. 32—White, Rose madder, Burnt sienna.

No. 33—White, Chrome-yellow (light), Yellow ochre.

No. 34—Chrome-yellow (deep), Terre verte, White.

No. 35—White, Red ochre, Chrome-yellow (light), Veronese green.

No. 36—White, Chrome-yellow (deep), Chrome-green (light).

No. 37—White, Prussian blue, Veronese green, Crimson lake.

No. 38—White, Chrome-yellow, (orange), Crimson lake, Raw sienna.

No. 39—White, Ultramarine (deep), Emerald-green.

No. 40—Madder lake (deep), White, Burnt umber.

In the following pages are given series of colour combinations in pairs or dyads, in sets of three or triads, in sets of four or tetrads. The author has tested in body colours all the combinations given.

The author does not claim each combination to be a model of perfection, but all of them can be employed successfully in decorative art.

DYADS or PAIRS OF COLOURS AFFORDING AGREEABLE COMBINATIONS.

1—Yellow, Violet.

2—Yellow (light), Turquoise.

3—Yellow, Purple.

4—Yellow (deep), Ultramarine.

5—Orange, Blue.

6—Orange-yellow, Violet.

7—Orange-yellow, Blue.

8—Orange, Turquoise.

9—Orange, Blue-grey.

10—Scarlet, Blue.

11—Vermilion, Turquoise.

12—Red, Blue.

13—Red (deep), Medium grey.

14—Green, Pink.

15—Brown, Warm green.

16—Black, Yellow.

17—Red, Blue-green.

18—Blue-green, Orange-red.

19—Scarlet, Buff.

20—Crimson, Yellowish-green.

21—Purple, Greenish-yellow.

22—Dark green, Orange.

23—Blue-green, Orange-yellow.

24—Terra cotta, Cream.

25—Havane, Blue (medium).

TRIADS OR THREE COLOURS AFFORDING AGREEABLE COMBINATIONS.

1—Orange, Green, Violet.

2—Violet, Scarlet, Olive green.

3—Yellow, Purple, Green.

4—Blue, Yellow, Red.

5—Sea green, Venetian red, Chamois.

6—Grey-blue, Lemon, Greenish-gold.

7—Indigo, Orange-red, Yellow (deep).

8—Ultramarine, Coral, Lemon.

9—Orange, Light blue, Stone (light).

10—Blue, Yellow orange, Turquoise.

11—Orange-red, Dark blue-green, Greyish-yellow-green.

12—Dark blue, Amber, Olive green.

13—Crimson, Cream, Dark greenish-yellow.

14—Moss green, Pink, Orange (pale).

15—Dark crimson, Havane, Blue (light).

16—Green (dark), Violet, Orange-yellow.

17—Orange, Lavender, Yellowish-green.

18—Ruby, Green-gold, Blue.

19—Grey-green, Lemon (deep), Purple.

20—Black, Orange, Greenish-blue.

TETRADS OR FOUR COLOURS AFFORDING AGREEABLE COMBINATIONS.

1.
Sea green.
Red.
Greenish-yellow.
Dark grey.

2.
Ultramarine.
Orange (pale).
Olive green (dark).
Violet.

3.
Crimson.
Cream.
Pink.
Grey-green.

4.
Turquoise.
Venetian red.
Blue-green.
Citrine gold.

5.
Dark blue.
Yellow-orange (pale).
Cream.
Turquoise.

6.
Umber.
Olive green (warm).
Indigo.
Grey-blue.

7.
Violet.
Gold.
Red.
Blue.

8.
Deep brown.
Lemon yellow.
Olive green.
Grass green.

9.
Greyish-green.
Stone (light).
Red.
Bluish-green.

10.
Gold.
Blue.
Deep yellow.
Blue-green.

11.

Red amber.

Olive green.

Violet-purple.

Ultramarine.

13.

Orange.

Blue-grey.

Warm white.

Pea green.

12.

Slate blue.

Pompeian red.

Yellowish-green.

Pale orange-grey.

14.

Leaf green.

Orange (pale).

Pink (pale).

Terra cotta.

15.

Ruby red.

Blue (deep).

Greenish-gold.

Yellowish-green (light).

TABLE OF AGREEABLE CONTRASTS.

1—Apple green,	Salmon pink.
2—Deep blue,	Yellowish-green.
3—Ultramarine,	Dark yellow (greenish).
4—Indigo,	Orange.
5—Black,	Sage green.
6—Deep crimson,	Myrtle green.
7—Pompeian red,	Grey-green (yellowish).
8—Maroon,	Moss green.
9—Violet,	Amber.
10—Purple brown,	Buff.
11—Violet,	Bronze green.
12—Silver grey,	Light golden ochre.
13—Greyish slate-blue,	Grey-green (yellowish).
14—Dull orange,	Blue-grey.
15—Deep red,	Renaissance grey.
16—Deep crimson,	Yellowish-green.
17—Scarlet,	Turquoise.
18—Olive green,	Amber (dark).
19—Yellow,	Violet.
20—Fumed oak,	Olive green.
21—Heliotrope,	Lemon yellow.
22—Pearl grey,	Golden ochre.
23—Chocolate,	Sage green.
24—Dark green,	Drab.
25—Coral red,	Turquoise.
26—Maroon,	Bluish sage-green.
27—Red,	Neutral grey.

28—White,   Pink.

29—Plum,   Spring green.

30—Blue-green,   Grey-brown (neutral).

31—Slate,   Citrine.

32—Cream,   Greens and purples.

33—Olive,   Lavender.

A. DESAINT.

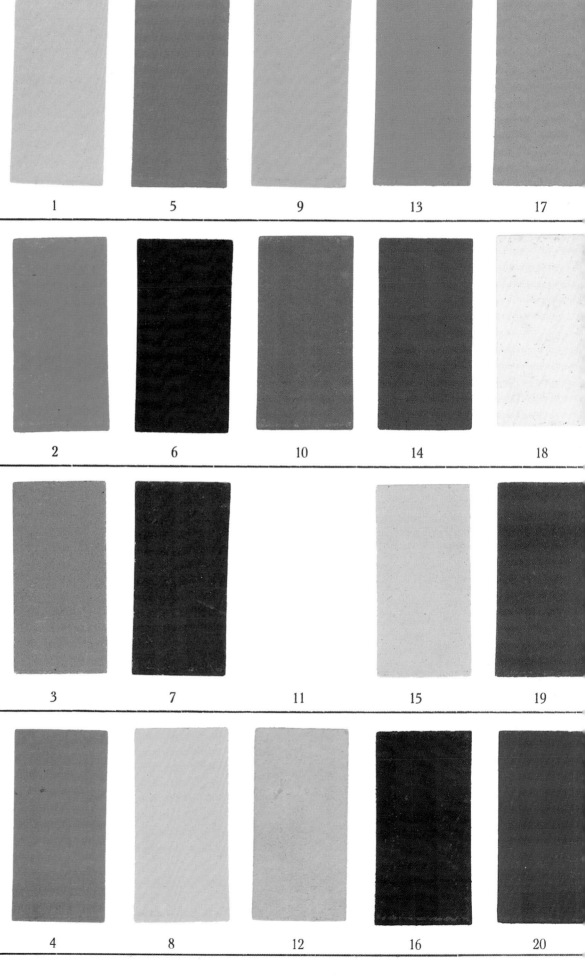

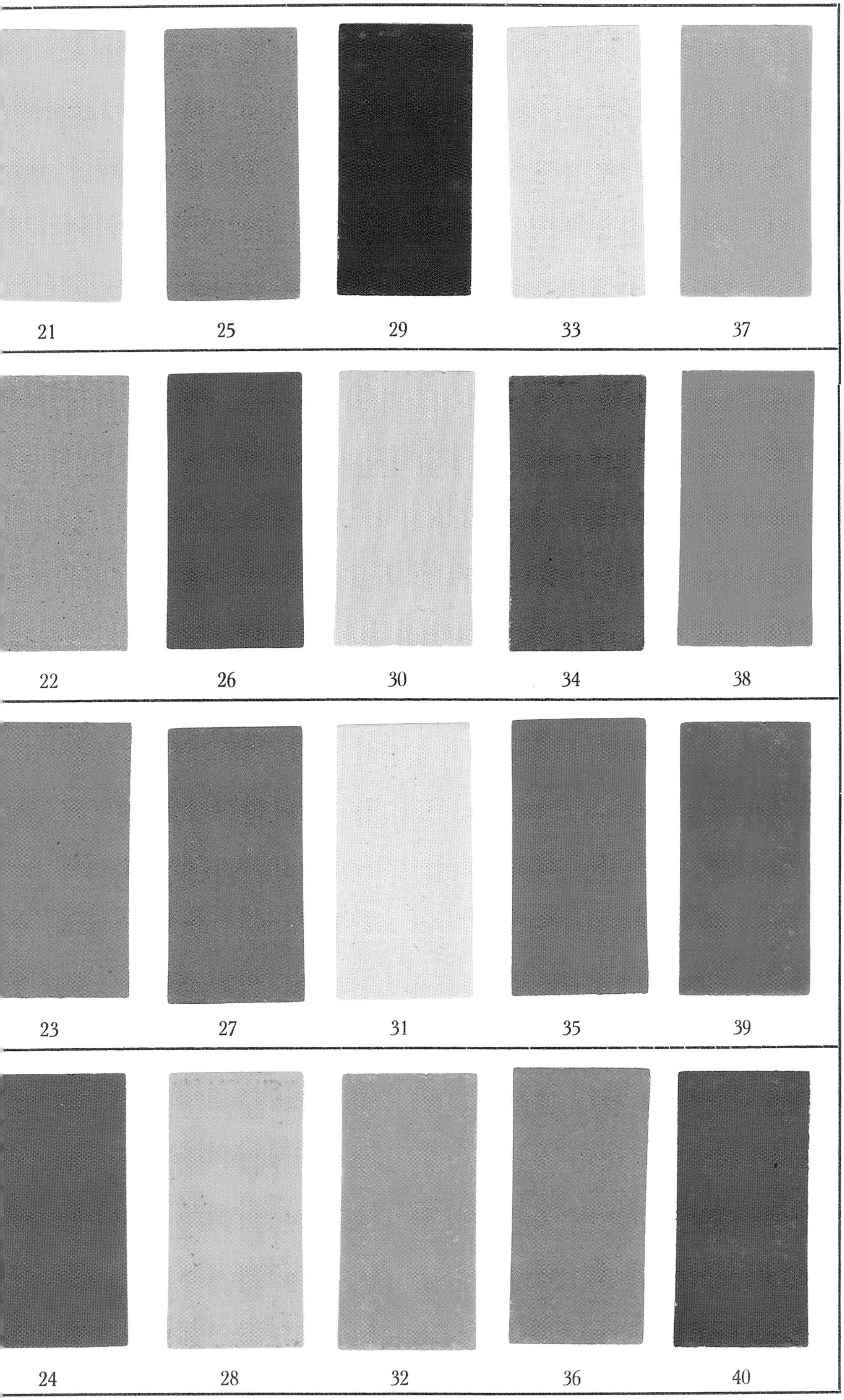

21

25

29

33

37

22

26

30

34

38

23

27

31

35

39

24

28

32

36

40

Plate II   Coloration 37-38-39-40.   Desaint's Stencilling,

Plate III   Coloration : 29 - 30 - 31 - 32.   : Desaint's Stencilling

Plate IV   Colorations :

Desaint's Stencilling

4

Plate V   Colorations   Desaint's Stencilling

1° 21 22 23 24
11° 12 19 1 3

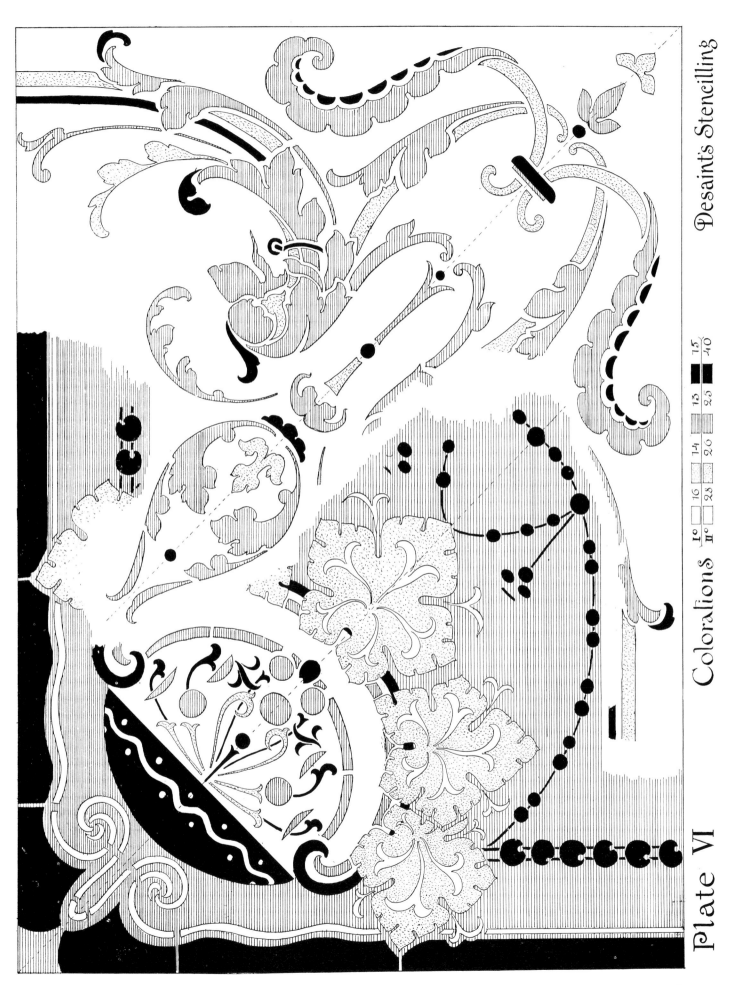

Plate VI   Colorations   Desaint's Stencilling

Plate VII   Colorations   Desaint's Stencilling

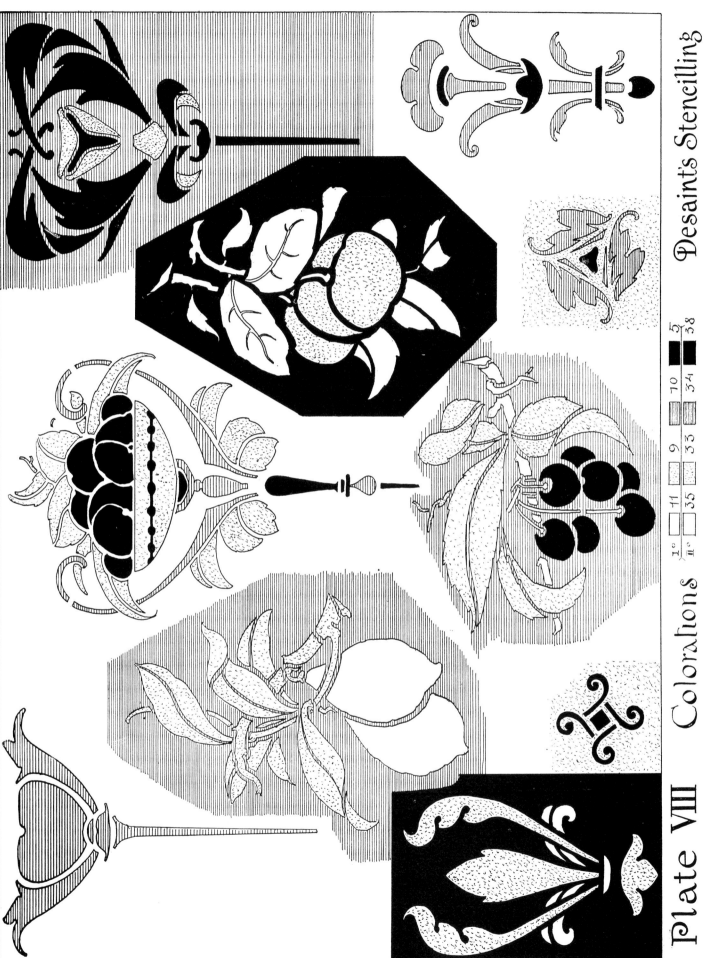

Plate VIII Colorations Desaint's Stencilling

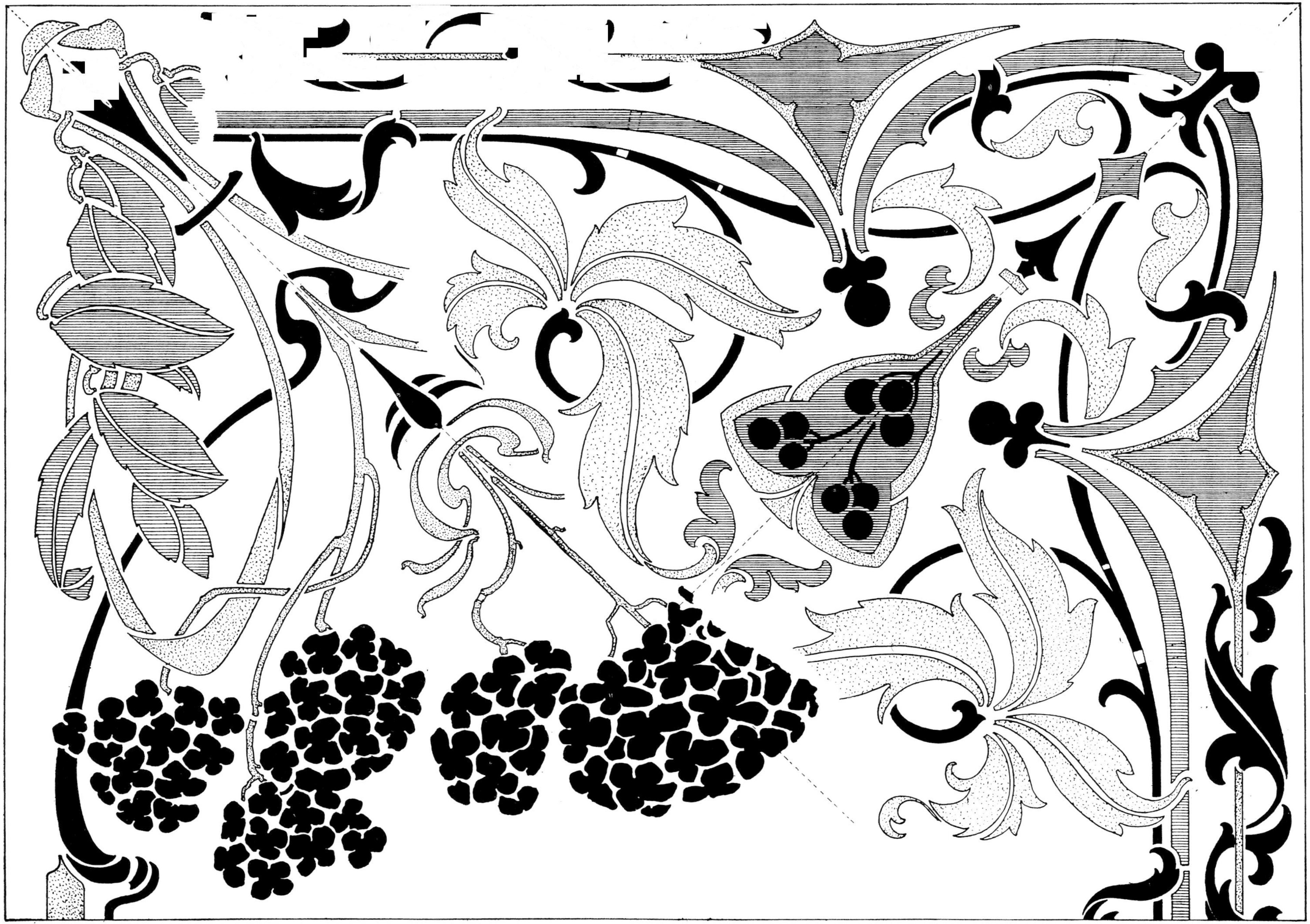

Plate IX — Colorations 1st: 7, 8, 14, 5; 2nd: 15, 19, 16, 17 — Desaint's Stencilling

Plate X Colorations Desaint's Stencilling

Plate XI   Colorations   Desaint's Stencilling

Plate XII

Colorations

1°	25	31	7	10
1°	12	2	37	56

Desaint's Stencilling

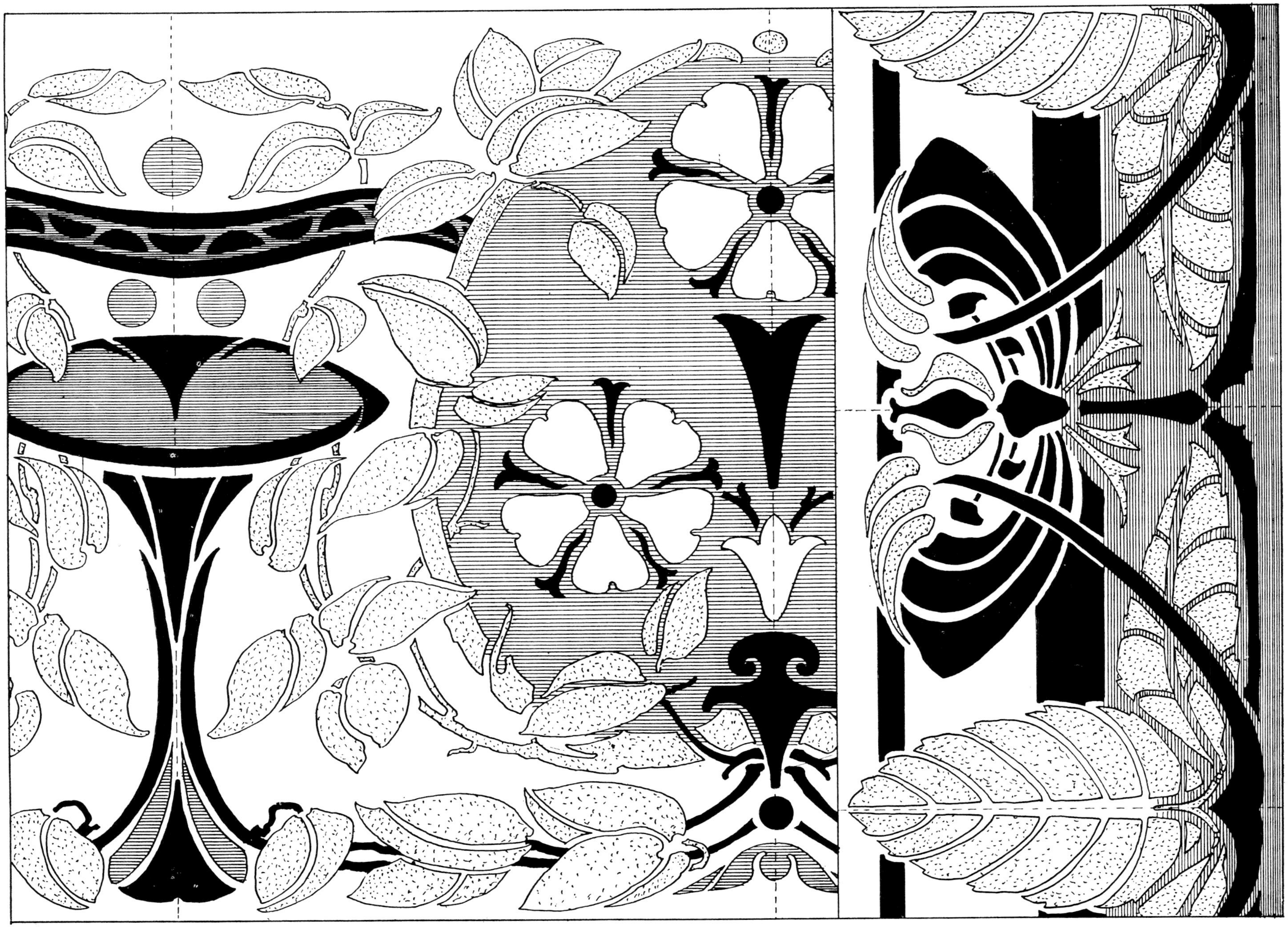

Plate XIII Colorations

I°	4	32	8	6
II°	13	7	35	20

Desaint's Stencilling

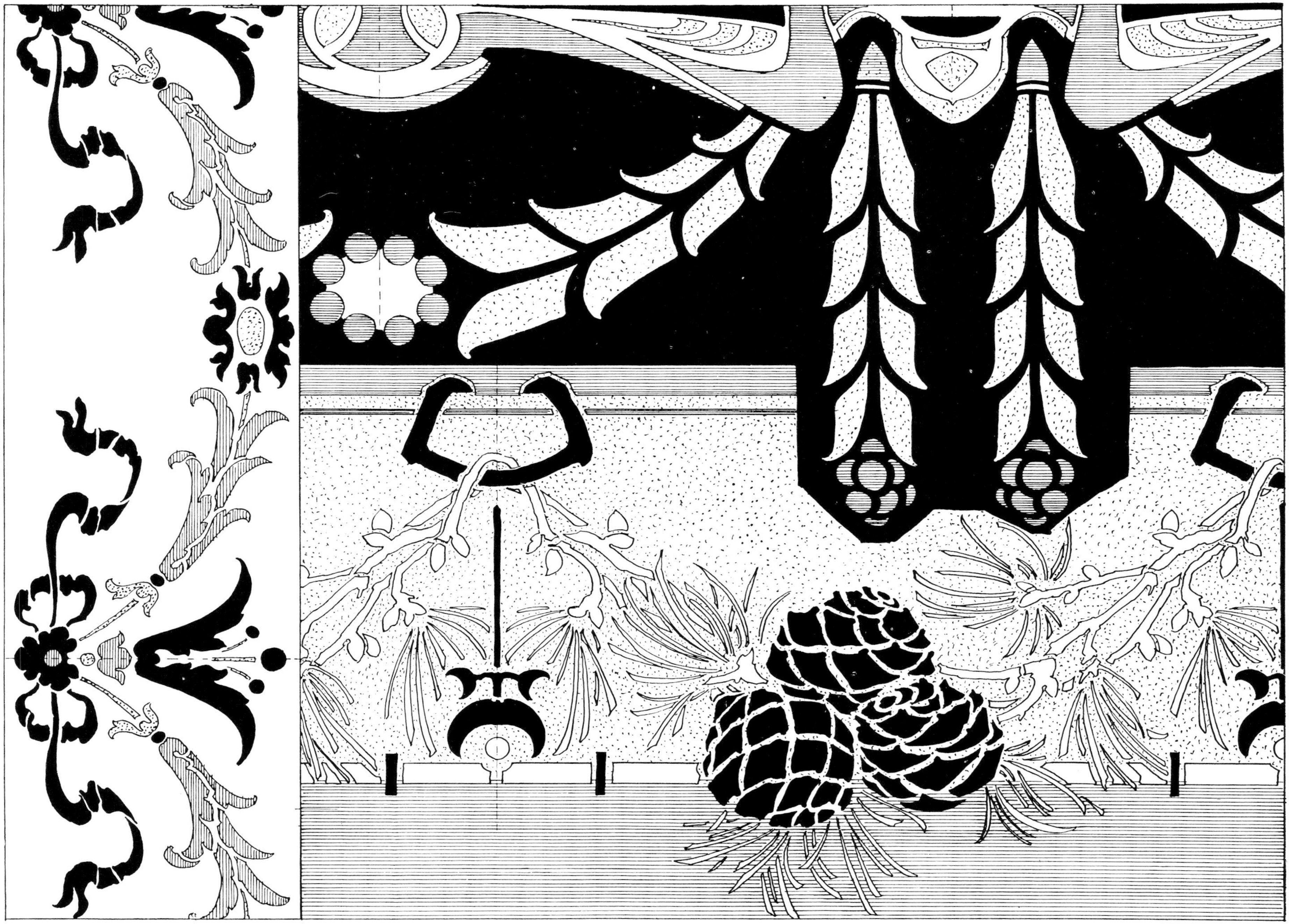

Plate XIV

Colorations

Desaint's Stencilling

Plate XV

Colorations

Plate XVI

Colorations

Desaint's Stencilling

Plate XVII   Colorations   Desaint's Stencilling

Plate XVIII

Colorations

Desaint's Stencilling

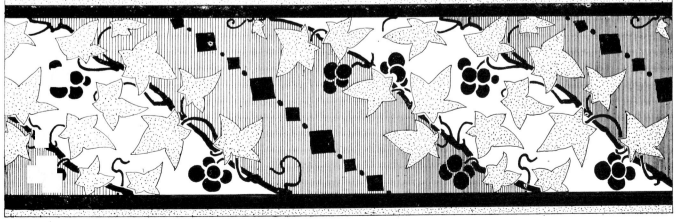

Plate XIX   Colorations   Desaint's Stencilling

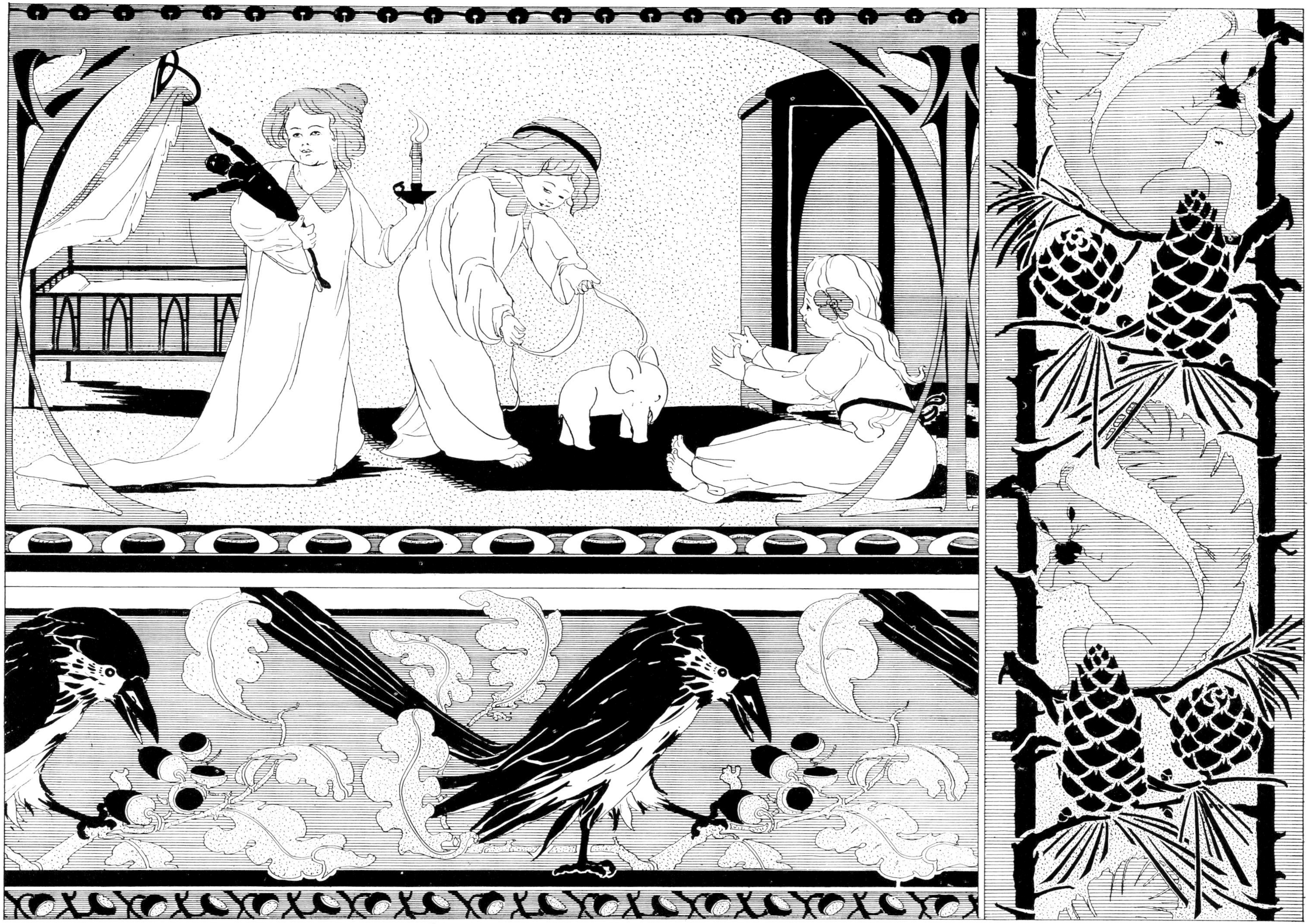

Plate XX — Colorations I° 31, 30, 32, 29; II° 21, 23, 24, 16 — Desaint's Stencilling

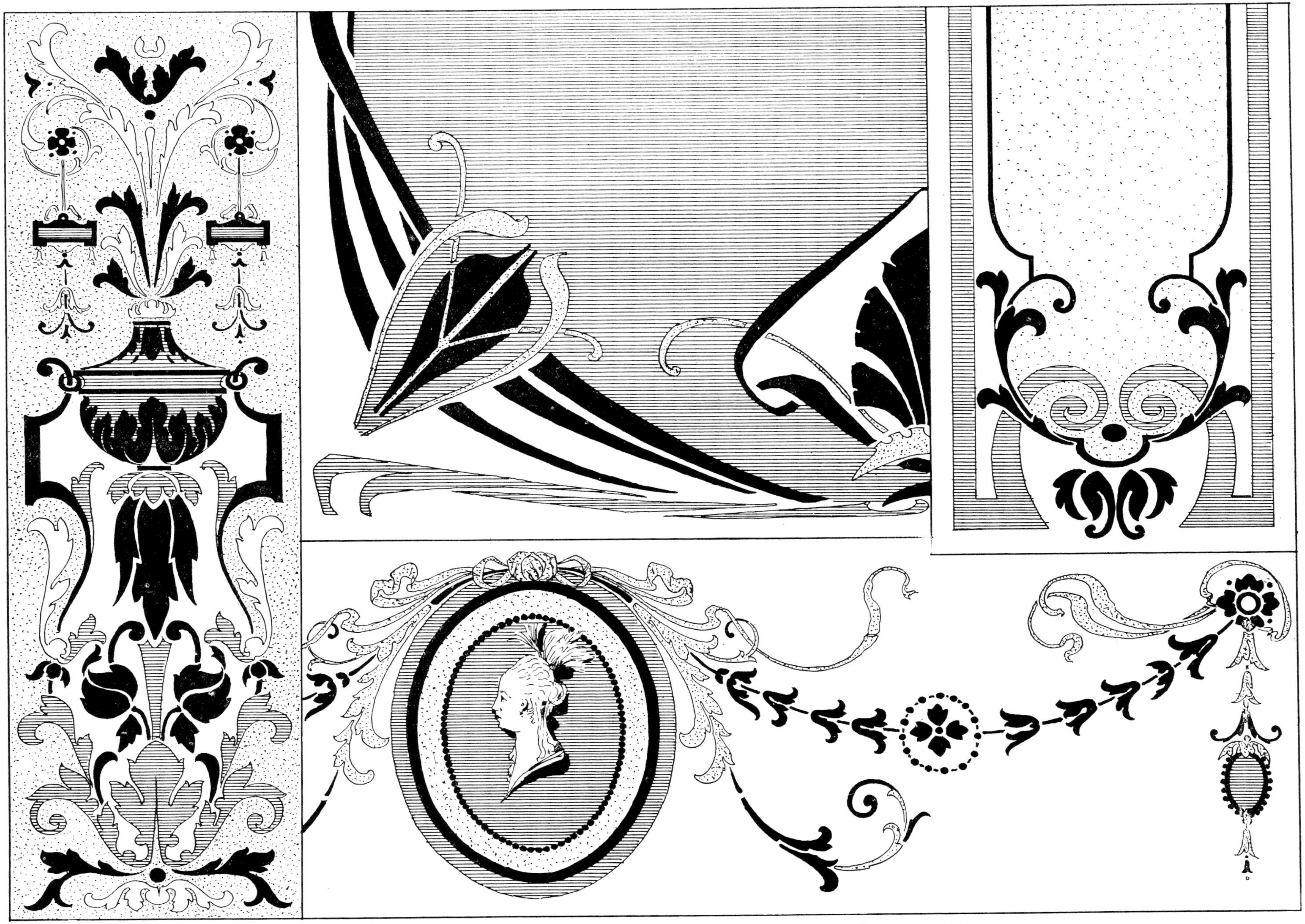

Colorations

Plate XXI   Desaint's Stencilling

Colorations

r°		12	17	19	20
II°		13	14	15	26

Desaint's Stencilling

Plate XII

7

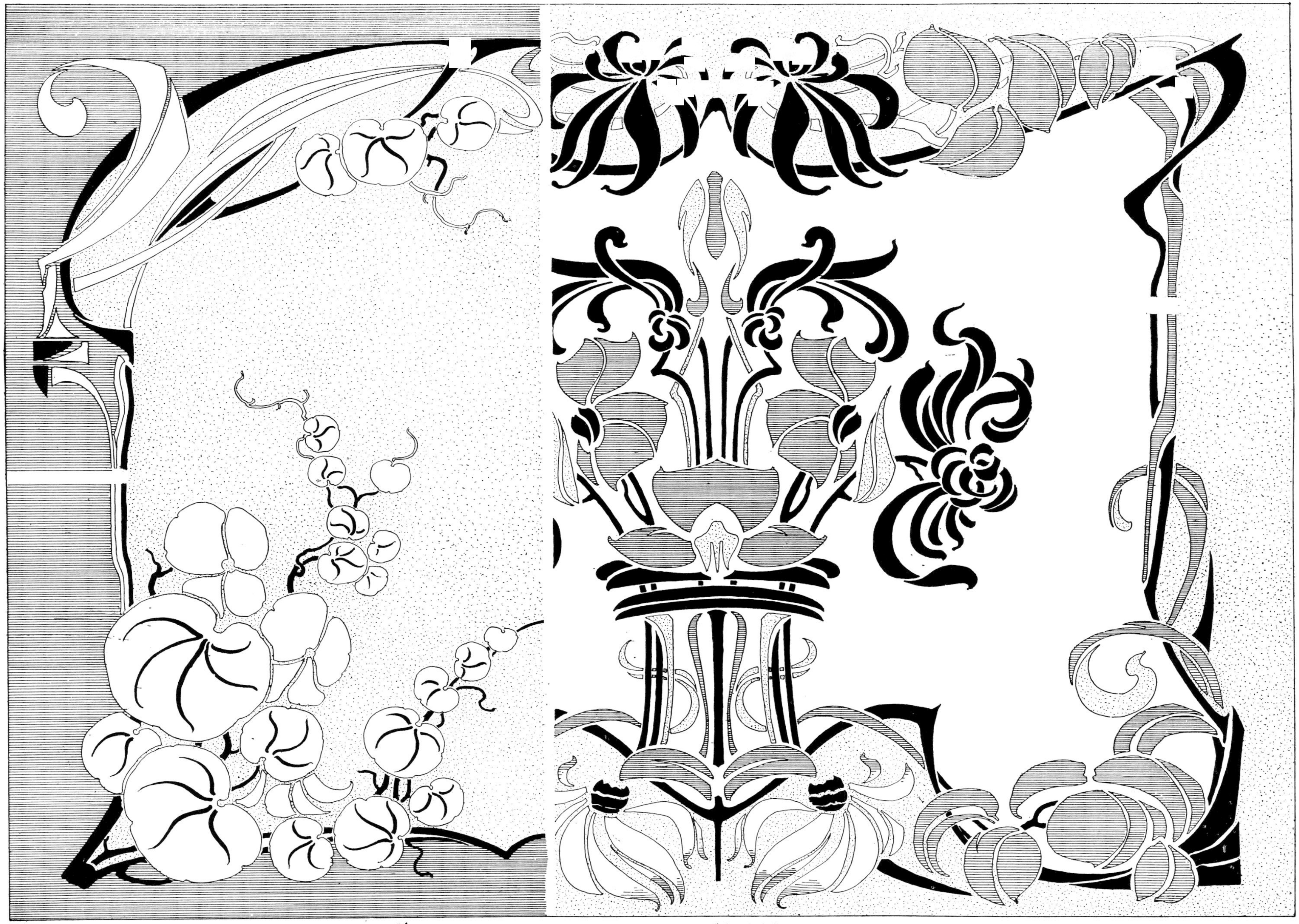

Plate XXIII Colorations I° 18, 22, 25, 40; II° 32, 33, 36, 34 Desaint's Stencilling

Colorations

| | | 13 | 14 | 15 | 17 |
| | | 10 | 11 | 12 | 16 |

Plate XXIV Colorations Desaint's Stencilling

Plate XXV Colorations Desaint's Stencilling

Plate, XXVI

Colorations

1°	30	17	27	29
II°	28	4	36	6

Desaint's Stencilling

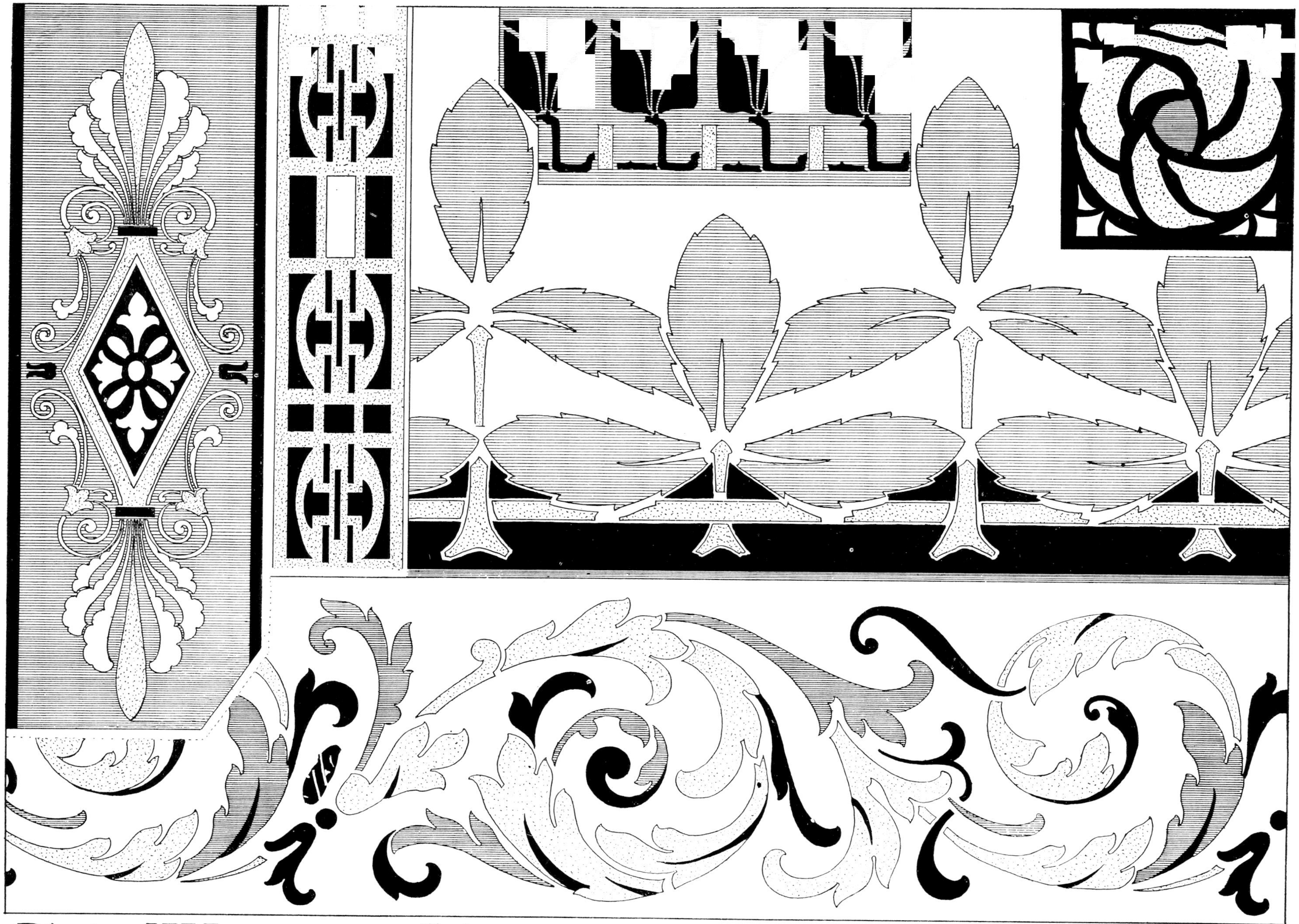

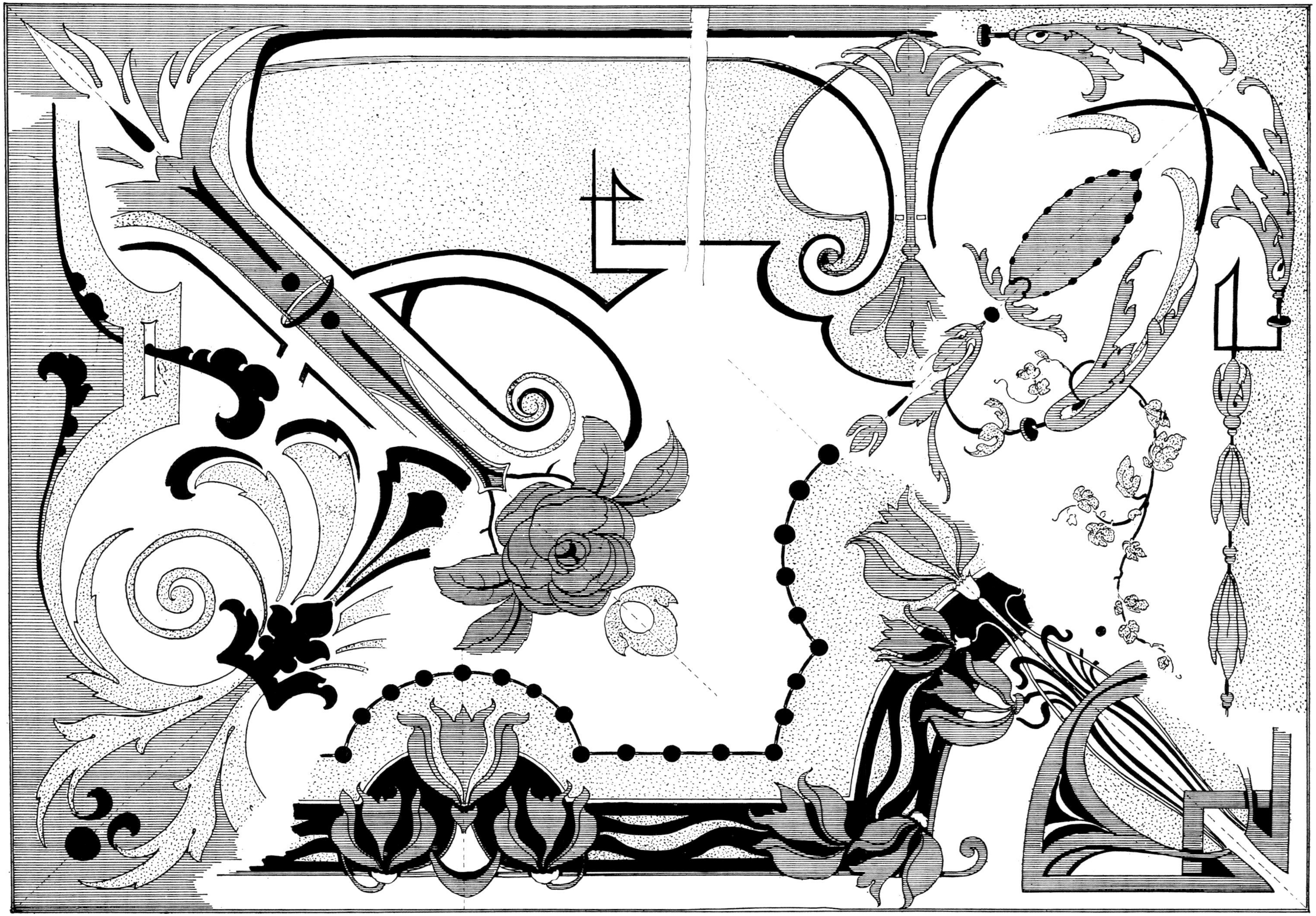

Plate XXVII

Colorations

I°	33	37	17	40
II°	12	35	14	38

Desaint's Stencilling

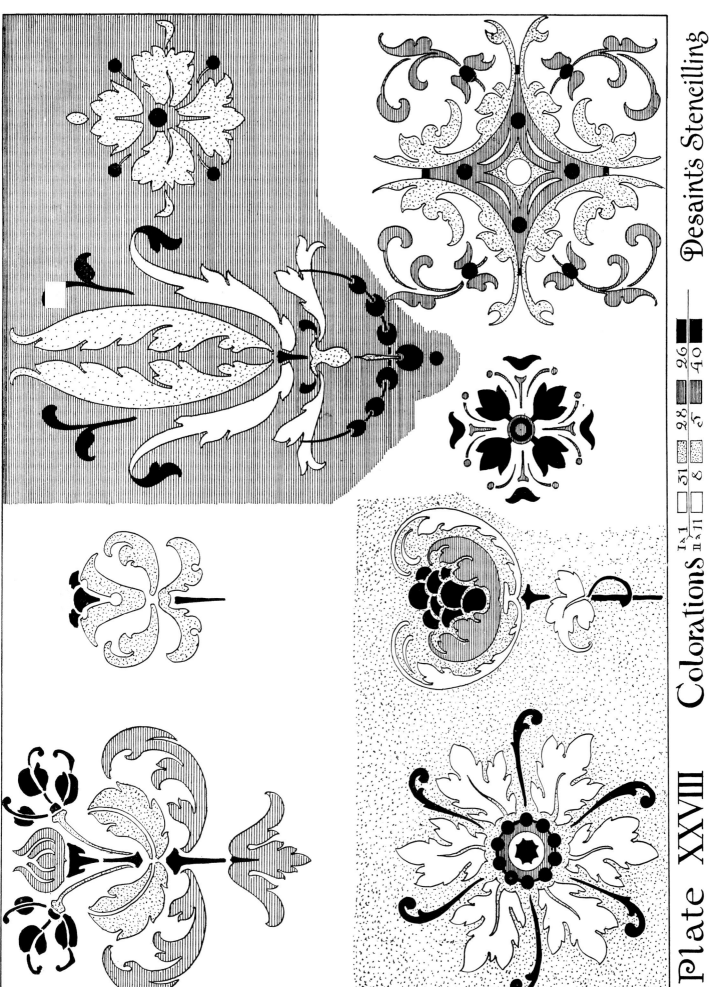

Plate XXVIII   Colorations $_{\text{II}\lambda\text{J1}}^{\text{I}\lambda\text{1}}$ Desaint's Stencilling

Plate XXIX   Coloration   Desaint's Stencilling

Colorations

I° ☐ 15 ▨ 3 ▨ 13 ■ 6
II° ☐ 20 ☐ 30 ▨ 19 ■ 18

Desaint's Stencilling

Plate XXX

8

Plate XXXI   Colorations   Desaint's Stencilling

Plate XXXII Colorations

I° ☐ 33 ☐ 35 ▦ 36 ■ 34
II° ☰ 7 ▥ 5 ▩ 8 ■ 6

Desaint's Stencilling

Plate XXXIII

Colorations 1° 2° 21 9 22 38 26 8 25 28

Desaint's Stencilling

Plate XXXIV   Colorations   Desaint's Stencilling

Plate XXXV

Colorations

I^o	39	37	33	11
II°	25	27	1	16

Desaint's Stencilling

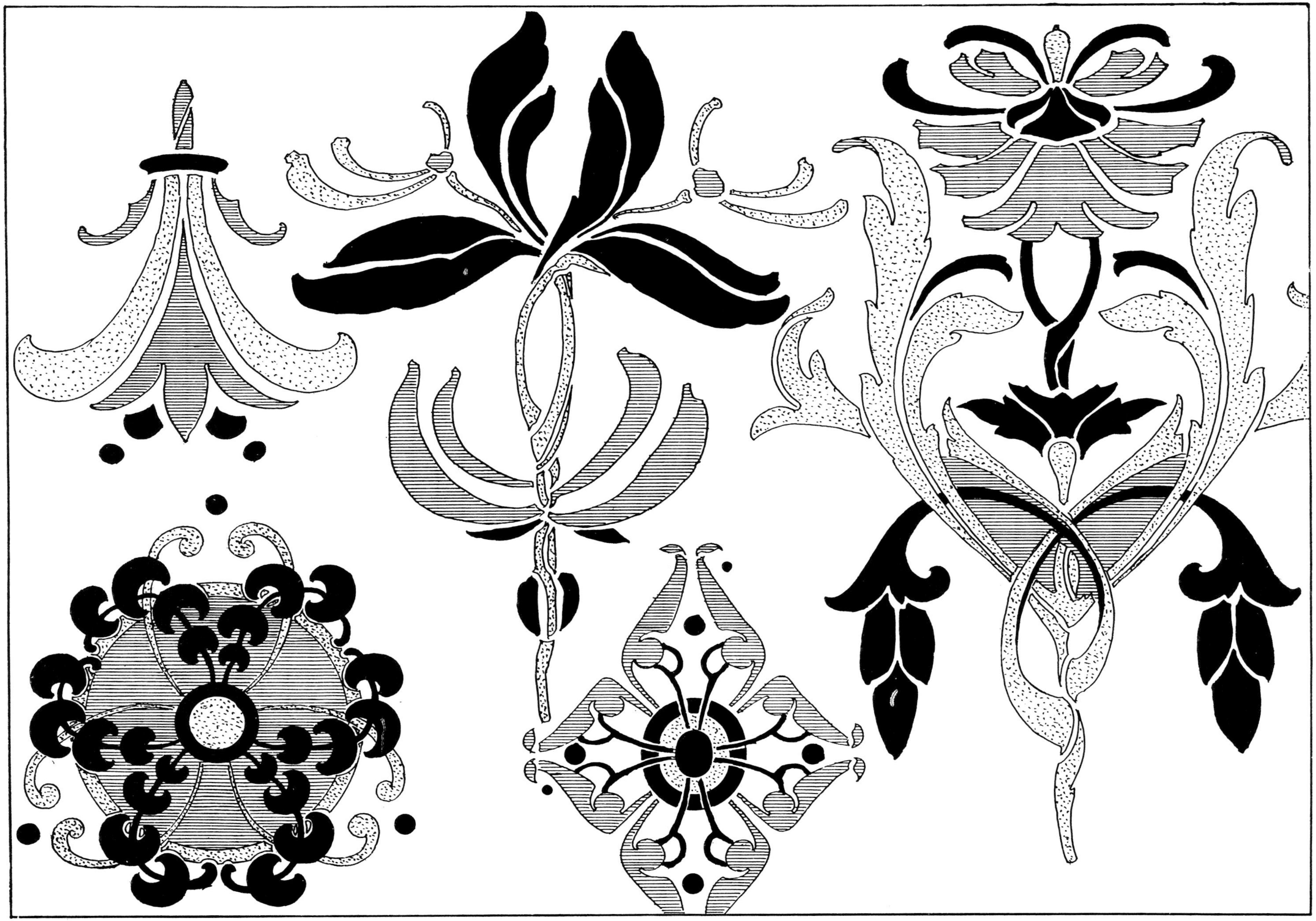

Plate XXXVI　　Colorations　　Desaint's Stencilling

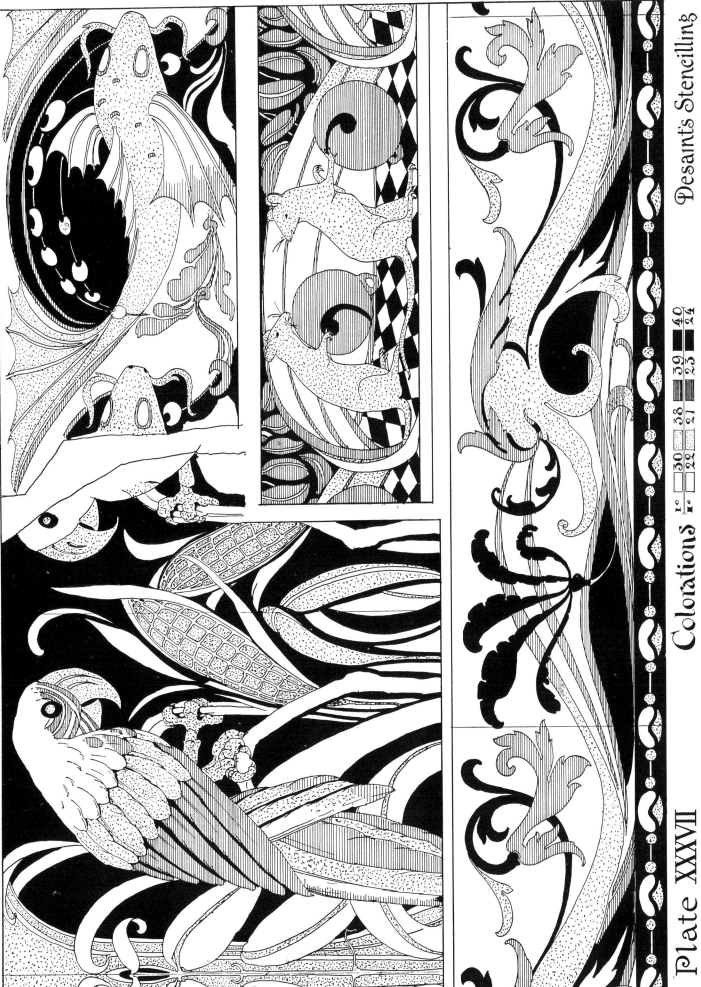

Plate XXXVII   Colorations   Desaint's Stencilling

Plate XXXVIII   Colorations   Desaint's Stencilling

9

Plate XXXIX

Colorations

| I.e | 13 | 14 | 15 | 16 |
| II.e | 34 | 37 | 28 | 31 |

Desaint's Stencilling

Colorations

I°	6	5	21	15
II	39	17	37	12

Plate XL

Desaints Stencilling